AF430386

Foreword

Every one of us has a dream; something we've always wanted to happen or accomplish.

It could be a career, a place to travel to, an attainable object, a personal evolvement of some kind.

I hope you know that your reality doesn't always have to stay your reality. You have the power to change anything you don't like and decide to do things differently. And you don't need anyone else to encourage you to do so. We have an incredible power within us; our passion and desire for personal growth.

"Going Beyond" is about looking deep into ourselves and finding what we want regardless of our current circumstance. We cannot change others, but we can take steps to change ourselves. And you are the only person who can figure out what you want to be happy.

I encourage you to embark on your own journey to really get to know yourself and always remember to have fun and enjoy yourself along the way!

Much love,

Isabella Evangeline

Dedicated
to all
Who feel different
Unusual
Not the norm
Don't worry
You're okay
Love yourself
Look in the mirror
Accept
Don't be labeled.
Just go out
And enjoy
The beautiful life
You've been given.

It takes **30 days** to incorporate a change…………….

The most beautiful gift is when one decides to love you.

But will you know

When

this happens……

Attachment

I want to experience
Love
Without
Attachment.
Letting it
Marinate
Grow
and form
on its own
without force.
Give it a chance
to become
what it's meant to
without being in
full control.

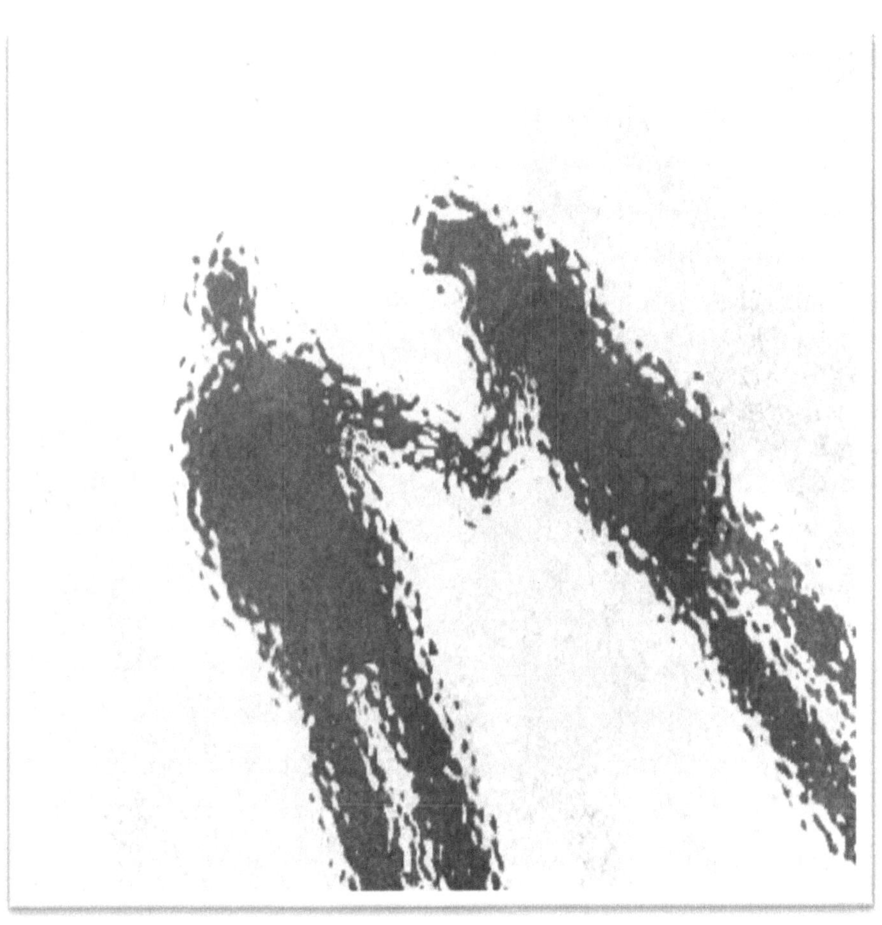

Unraveled

Tough as nails
she held it all in
as the only one
she could trust was
herself.
Living her life
free of stress
worry
Everyday
a blissful state.
And then she saw
Him
and un
        rave
            led.

You

You will never know
how I feel
because I won't tell you.
When I'm alone
I envision
Lavishing
You
with my overflowing heart
my affections.

But the moment I see you
    I freeze
I fear this hold you have on me
Get angry that I'm so...
vulnerable
so I do the opposite.

The Man

How hard it must be
to hold in your emotions
to be led astray
by your body
Not your mind.
Easily distracted
by a tantalizing carrot
a shiny object
instead of
Fighting for
priceless treasure.
A strong body
but a weaker mind
feeling pressure
to hold it all together.

But remember
a man never abandons
a woman he loves.

touch

Just hold my hand
and don't say a word
Just listen
Wholeheartedly
to my cries
Open up to me
with your dreams
Your fears
And take my breath away...

window

There is a window
if you are willing
to climb the distance.
It's not easy to get to
and risky
But hopefully what
You will see
will be worth it....

There's a fine line between

joy and sadness....

eyes wide open

Let's see
what the world
has to offer
No judgments
just facts
Truth.
I have to go
Discover
gather
Knowledge.
Wisdom
is intoxicating
I want to know
Understand
See.

Skin

My eyes hold my secrets
waiting to shed
Weathered skin
I've chosen
to carry
for the longest time.
I grew comfortable
in the corner
figuring it out
Myself
'till a little light
shined on me
and drew me out
to play.

standing still

Why can't
Time freeze
so I get a moment
to wander around
the corridor
of my life.
To take off
my mask
To hug
all the people
I love
To note
what I like
what I don't
what I want
to change.

the two selves

You are watching
Patiently observing
without judgment
As I leap...
Unhinged emotions
Mindless chatter
You see me
stumble over
obstacles
Waiting
for you
to guide me along.
I need you
to fill in the gaps
I cannot see
Blurred vision
I'm moving too fast
to see the
Truth.

My Mercy

Prevails

Over

My wrath

The chase

He ignores
I find it mysterious
Enchanting.
It's a puzzle
That can't be solved
It grabs my attention
Keeps me guessing.
But why do I want something
Not worth having?

Withdrawal

Something is missing
i am not the same
my vision is darkened
my soul is cloudy
my body aches.
I feel this pull
Pushing you away
I can't bear it
it tears me in two.
Half of me wants
to run to you
to feel safe
in your arms.
Half of me wants
to fight you
for stealing
my heart
from me.

Too late

I felt something
Deep
pierce me.
Struggling
to make sense
of it.
Working out the puzzle
in front of me.
So I pulled hard
but caught nothing
Frustrated
for not giving up.
Finally
I walked…..
Admitting defeat
Imagination
was my conclusion.
As I left running
You were racing to catch me.

Fight

Sometimes you need
your heart broken
Several times
to understand
what love is.
And when you
Find it again...
You will fight
Your hardest
to never let it go...

The pursuit of Perfection

Are we happier
when we focus
All our energy
upon looking a certain way to   Others
Chased by many
Envied by all
But inside   left
Unfulfilled...

Do we get up in the morning
Genuinely happy with our lives
Savoring each moment
with things that cost...
Nothing
Enjoying ourselves
Encouraging others
Grateful to experience love
Genuine care for others
and the peace that comes from Truth.

Bad things happen

to help you realize

how good things are...

One

Visiting new places
Different ways
of doing
Similar things
Delicacies
Customs
Culture
Religion
Identifiers
Separate.
But we are all
Human
One of the same.

the bird

She was on an island
all by herself
Everyday
she awoke to silence
Serenity
Peace.
She turned her fear
into wisdom
embracing the unknown.
At times
she longed for another
to remind her
of her existence.
And every morning
the bird landed on her shoulder
gave a little nod
then quickly flew off
leaving her to solitude.

the star

Wandering...
i was lost
Not physically
But spiritually.
Who could I trust
Who would love me
Enough
to tell me the truth?
Who would actually hear me
Not pretend to listen.
And then I looked up
And you twinkled
to remind me
that i was heard.

REJECTION

is an indicator

that it's not the best

relationship

for you.

Words

Please
Take the time
to really mean
what you say
and say
what you mean.
Our voice
is powerful
its unique
It can change
someone's life
for the worse
or for the
better.

Age

The old
are unappealing
Bodies weakened
by age
They cry out
Complain
But the young
would give anything
for an ounce
of their wisdom.

Overflowing

I am so full...
Happiness spills over
                    sprinkling onto people
                    as they pass me by.
I am so grateful
of who I am
and what I've become.
It's a tough world
I must take care
of myself first
without burdening others
so I can be strong enough
to pull the people
I love.

Legacy

The most beautiful thing
to witness
is growth
in others
Seeing a seed
that you've sprinkled
with your mentorship
watching it bloom
into a flower
with its very own garden.

With more Knowledge

comes more distress

The Wall

I keep
Ramming into it
Over and over
the same result.
Battered more
each time.
Why do I
Convince myself
to continue
this action
when all I need to do
is climb

          over it

and leave it   behind?

inside

Running in circles
I need to be still
Ponder
Alone
my options
my choices.
Yearning
for that inner voice
of wisdom
to tell me
a secret.
Patiently
Waiting
for me to
just
Listen.

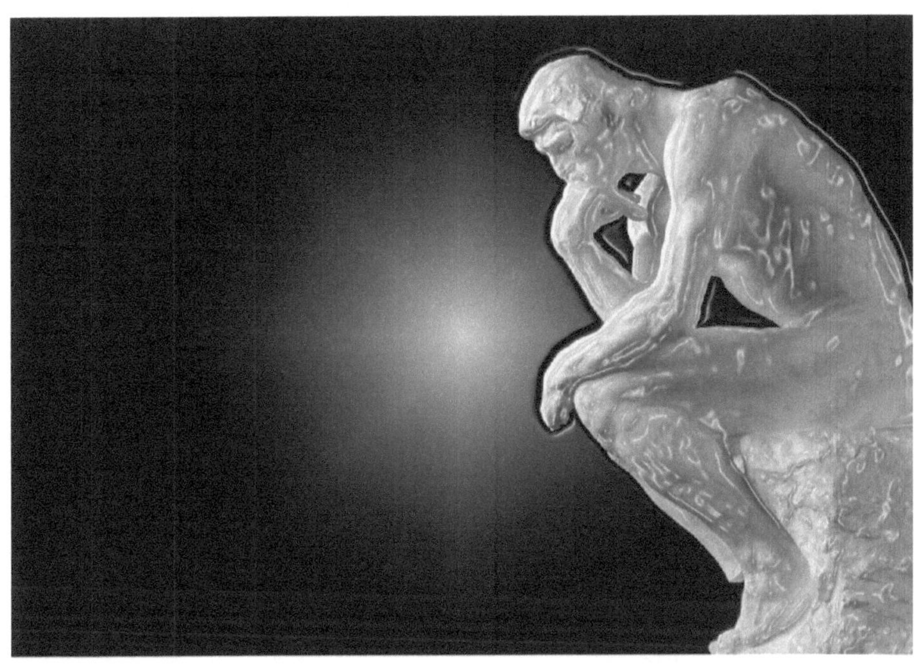

Freedom

I decide
if I choose
to be happy
or ungrateful
Always wanting more.

I decide
if I appreciate
my current circumstance
if I label it
good
or bad.

The world
is ever-changing
Unpredictable
like a weathering storm.
Don't let it determine
who you are.

Color

In the mirror
I looked
as if meeting myself
for the first time.
I saw the lines
of perseverance
The eyes of
Contentment
The smile of love
The dancing spirit
as the gray
turned to color.

Nobody

can break your heart

if you love yourself.

The Commitment

I desperately want you
to be the center of
My world
I imagine
You rescuing me
from everyone's wrath
their disappointment.
You being the light
Leading me
from darkness.
This twisted tale
is choking
the life
the love
Out of me
Unrealistic
Expectations
A stubborn dream
now a nightmare
Leaving me
in distress.

I will be
My own light
to shine
to sparkle
the good in me.
I will love myself
as devoted
as one can be
So I'm completely full

Never needing...
But wanting
another.

The Woman

I know it's hard...
to try to be it all
So much pressure
we put on ourselves
so we can be accepted
Admired
Chosen.
The image we want
The identity we fight to keep
The burden thrown on another.
Don't set yourself up
But choose yourself
First
Don't let others
Make this choice
For you.

Metamorphosis

Day by day
I decide
to act...
Differently.
Make new choices
Uncover stones
Untouched
Fish in
untraveled waters
Open wide
My eyes
My mind
30 days
My heart 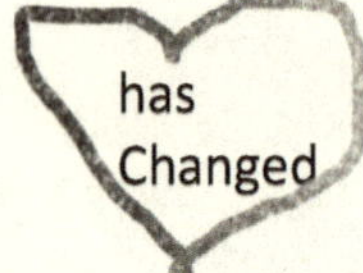

Beyond

I'm not stopping
I'm going to stretch myself
to the limits of
Personal growth.
When it gets hard
I'm going to push farther
Harder
because even though
No one is watching
I'm with myself
till the end
And I want to be happy
with the person I've become.

Find what you love to do and

EXPLORE

Acknowledgments

I am very grateful that I've met wonderful people during the course of my life and to have visited great inspiring places with hopefully more to come.

I wake up each day, like many of us, not knowing what interesting events will take place, what impactful people I will meet and learn from and what new discoveries I will unearth about myself. This state of discovery reminds me of having the heart of a child in such as adopting an adventurous spirit and really enjoying that precious free time we are given.

No matter what your circumstance is I encourage you to really embrace learning. It could be traveling, reading a book, adopting a new hobby, having a meaningful conversation with someone you know or don't, or just going for a walk and observing. Having a passion for learning opens your eyes to a whole new world and helps you uncover things you never knew about yourself.

And the more you learn about yourself, the more you learn about what makes you truly happy........and then your once distant dreams start to become your reality......